SPORTS LIFE BUSINESS: THE TRANSITION PLAYBOOK

SPORTS LIFE BUSINESS: THE TRANSITION PLAYBOOK

DERRICK FURLOW, JR.

SPORTS LIFE BUSINESS LLC

Copyright © 2017 by Derrick Furlow, Jr.
All rights reserved. Written permission must be secured from the publisher to use or reproduce any part of this book, except for brief quotations in critical reviews or articles.

Author photo and cover graphics provided by 360 MediaGroup.
Page layout by Win-Win Words LLC

Readers of this book are also encouraged to purchase the companion book, *What's Next? How to Transition Like a Champion,* **available at retail outlets, amazon.com, and www.sportslifebusiness.com.**

Impact, Inspire & Empower LLC (IIE), the source of some of the maxims included in this book, is registered by the author.

ISBN: 978-0-9992746-1-3

Printed in the United States of America

CONTENTS

	The Mission of the Transition PlayBook	7
	Pregame	11
1	How to Transition Like a Champion	17
2	Three Things You Can't Miss	25
3	Life Happens	33
4	The Choice Is Yours	41
5	Know the Game	49
6	The Transition	59
7	Master the Mind-set	69
8	The Basics: Reading, Writing & Arithmetic	77
9	Go Pro at Life	87
10	Raise the Bar	97
11	Audible: Check Omaha, Riverside	105
	About the Author	113

THE MISSION OF THE TRANSITION PLAYBOOK

THIS COURSE WILL TAKE THE INTANGIBLE SKILLS, PHILOSOPHIES, principles, and lessons you have learned in sports and show you how to apply them to your life or your business and create the tangible success you desire.

This curriculum was designed to show you two things: first, that you already possess the skills that will make you successful, and second, there are daily challenges you face and principles you encounter that, if learned, can be applied to various areas of your life. Whether it's in sports, life, or business, applying these principles will give you the ability to drastically shorten your learning curve and give you a distinct advantage in the marketplace of life and business. It will create a path to success in half the time.

I created this course to reveal to you that the knowledge you have learned from sports contains arguably all the winning-edge fundamentals you need for life and business. I have learned, seen, and used all of them. My hope is that you will recognize your unfair advantage in your sports arena, in life, and in business as you go through your journey. Through this curriculum, you will learn what most athletes/people do not learn until it is too late and yet they need to know it. Study and practice these philosophies because they represent the winning edge that will take you from where you are in sports, life, or business to where you want to be—if they are applied correctly and consistently.

We make our biggest mistakes in life when we don't apply the lessons we have learned. We go through every endeavor with the intent of experiencing a flawless outcome, hoping to make minimal mistakes along the way. But we often don't take the time to apply our acquired knowledge to sports, life, or business. The kicker is that most of us are not conscious of these lessons. We don't take the time to reflect on how they can benefit us long after we have learned them. There won't be any excuse after you complete this course. In fact, after taking this course, you will no longer be able to say, "I didn't think about that" or "I didn't know what to do." You will be more aware that whatever you are encountering now, there is always something you will have endured, experienced, heard about, or even read that you can apply to help you achieve your desired goals.

COURSE OBJECTIVES

1. Reveal to you the skills, lessons, principles, and philosophies that sports can teach you.

2. Demonstrate how sports has embedded in you the skill set, lessons, principles, and philosophies that you need to succeed in life and business.

3. Show you how to take the intangible skills, lessons, principles, and philosophies from sports and begin to apply them to create tangible results in life and business.

4. Help you transition that champion's mind-set from your sport into the game of life and business.

5. Show you how to put these skills, lessons, principles, and philosophies into action in every phase of sports, life, and business.

COURSE DESCRIPTION

This course will provide the principles, philosophies, and mind-set you need to excel in sports, in life, and in business. These are the exact same principles and philosophies you used in athletics and that are used by athletes around the world. Some of them then went on to use these principles and philosophies to transition and succeed in their personal lives and business endeavors.

In this course, we will review general concepts that highlight intangible skills used in sports competition. The intent here is to help you discover the correlation between sports, life, and business instead of just hearing about it. Finally, the goal is to help you break through and get the trash out, so you can live the life you want beyond sports.

PREGAME

LET'S SET THE TONE, BEFORE WE GET INTO IT. *STOP*. TAKE HOWEVER much time you need to *relax* and *breathe*!! Just know you will be all right. The fear, the worry, the doubt, the depression, the shame, whatever it is that you might be feeling at this moment, let it go. Realize this: it is all self-inflicted—no one is controlling your pain but you. The sooner you let it go, the sooner you can move forward.

The first thing you must do to move forward during your transition is to release yourself from "identity jail." Identity jail is where you can only see yourself as an athlete or n whatever role you have been in until this point in your life. Stop holding yourself hostage to the only identity you know of yourself and explore your new reality. Athletes can find themselves in identity jail for as brief a time as one year to as long as a life sentence, depending on their mind-set after playing the game. The longer you wait in identity jail, the higher your bond will be to get you out. This program will reduce that time by 50 percent if applied properly. If you are ready to be free, let's begin.

In the same way you developed yourself to see yourself as an athlete, now you must develop yourself to see yourself as something else. You must reintroduce yourself to yourself because you don't know yourself as anyone else. I remember turning into "Derrick the businessman" and no longer being "Derrick the athlete."

You must reintroduce yourself to the world as a nonathlete, because those who know you don't know you as anything but an athlete. It will be scary, but it must be done. Until you can see yourself in a new light as someone different, no one else will. Do not depend on others for confirmation; your self-perception will be your confirmation.

Believe in yourself. You can do it. If you don't believe in yourself, why would anyone else believe in you?

PREGAME WARMUP

The Hollis Project

Make a list of WHO you are without your sport:

1. I am _____

2. I am _____

3. I am _____

4. I am _____

5. I am _____

6. I am _____

7. I am _____

8. I am _____

9. I am _____

10. I am _____

SPORTS LIFE BUSINESS
THE TRANSITION PLAYBOOK

1
HOW TO TRANSITION LIKE A CHAMPION

WE USE THE PHRASE "TRANSITION LIKE A CHAMPION" WITH ALL sincerity. The transition process for most people is a crucial part of their lives and has a huge effect on their success. Maybe it doesn't have a significant effect on overall success, but it definitely does on how they start that next chapter during the transition and how long it takes them to start anew. The transitional success I had played a key role in my being where I am today. I also know the transitional roles—some good, some bad—that my teammates held also played a critical role for them. That's why I felt it only right to enlighten you on how to transition like a champion. This is so you can put yourself and others in a winning position before, during, and after your transition.

Directions: As you go through each section of this book, make the correlation to how each concept relates to you, then figure out how you can apply each in your sport, your life, and your business.

CARRYOVER

First things first: carryover. The law of carryover also can be described as the "same-as principle." The idea behind this principle is comparing the new path to the previous path. The fastest way to do this is to correlate: "This is the same as that." You might say, "What I bring to my new field (endeavor) is the same as what I took from my old field in the game of sports." This is where the magic happens. (Remember, "This is the same as that.")

Carryover also breeds the premise that once you're successful on the field, you can take that success and those exact same principles or psychology that made you successful and carry them over to another field. When doing so, you should produce the same outcome—success!

Before executing carryover, think of past successes, principles, philosophies, psychology, and the things that worked for you or against you.

You do not want to carry over any bad principles, philosophies, or psychology you might have, so it's critical you take the time to do a self-assessment. Take inventory and make a list of what worked for you and what didn't, so you can weed out the latter.

The biggest secret behind the carryover is taking those principles, philosophies, and lessons you learned and which worked when applied to the game, and now apply them to the new you and your new chapter.

THE SAME OLD PRINCIPLES, BUT A NEW YOU

In my book *What's Next? How to Transition Like a Champion*, I offer multiple examples of the skills I used, which I call "carryover." Even then, there still is a learning curve to some degree in terms of carrying over principles, but it's minimal, making the odds of having success almost inescapable. The question becomes, what principles did you learn from the game? Do you remember how you applied them? Which ones can you apply here and now?

You can usually find the answers from your own experiences, but a good Plan B is reading my book, *What's Next?* That is exactly what Sports, Life & Business (SLB) is designed to do: show you how to recognize and apply the intangible lessons, skills, principles, and philosophies you need to carry over that which will make you wildly successful in sports, life, or business!

THERE IS POWER IN PERSPECTIVE

Your perspective is everything. It will either help you or hurt you. But you are the one who picks it, so choose wisely.

Do not let irrelevant perspectives or realities impact, dictate, or control your realities or perspectives. Don't let what is going on in someone else's world or their thoughts control your world.

A lot of times you might feel people are judging you because you did not make it to that next level, whatever the next level was for you. But deep down it's you judging yourself; it's you projecting that perspective of failure out onto the world. So that unconfident energy and failure perspective is the same energy you are getting back from others.

"They" say you can control only your attitude, but I believe "they" are wrong. I believe you can also control your perspective! During your transition from sports to life and business, your perspective can create additional problems for you because you haven't taken the time to redefine yourself before transitioning.

The way you see things will play a major role in your attitude toward how things actually are, the actions you take, and your approach. Do you have the proper perspective? That is the question, and the answer is ultimately up to you. What I've found is that the proper perspective normally consists of, first, a bright-sided outlook—finding a way to see the good when everything looks bad. It's finding a positive, results-driven solution, not making excuses.

Throughout this program, you are learning how to dominate your thinking—this is not only so you can control your perspective, but also is how to change your perspective, which was influenced by how you viewed your environment.

For things to change, you must first change your perspective.

KNOW WHAT YOU KNOW

After all those years, months, weeks, days, and hours of practice and preparation for your sport, just know you are a pro at something. It has been said it takes ten thousand hours of practicing a skill to be considered a professional. Before you technically decide upon a profession, just know there are some skills for which you can be considered a pro based on the ten thousand hours concept. The question is, what skills have you practiced the most? In what skills do you feel you have invested ten thousand hours?

One of the key ingredients to moving forward and transitioning effectively is knowing what you know, what are you good at. You have mastered a skill set or some skills along the way relative to whatever it is that you did or that you are now doing, whether you believe it or not. You have developed confidence in that skill or those skills, but you probably do not recognize yourself as being a "pro" at them.

A good example is athletes and training; athletes physically train so much for their particular sport that they become good at it. Once they are done playing that sport, an easy transition is one that goes into the fitness, training, coaching world because they know what they know and have put thousands of hours of training in and around the gym. With me, it was making friends, or networking, having the ability to meet and connect with people. I had developed this during all the moving I did as a child and from making friends with all my teammates over the years of playing sports. Different people, different backgrounds, different sports, but I was able to make friends. By the time it was for me to make a transition from sports into life and the business world, I knew what I was a pro at—that was networking, which gave me confidence. I explain how that worked in *What's Next?* I knew what I knew.

Knowing my strengths and what I knew in terms of applicable skills (i.e. networking) made it easier for me when I got into sales. I gravitated toward positions that involved understanding people, which allowed me to carry over my networking skills I had worked on for years and mastered while in college. It also made it clear to me the things I needed to learn because my past hadn't offered any experience in those areas, or I failed to recognize the learning opportunities from my sport; which is normally the case for athletes. Life is not just knowing what you know, it's knowing what you don't know—it's a strong self-awareness. Knowing what I know was a game changer for me; it made me aware of the learning curve ahead (or lack thereof) as I transitioned.

Knowing what you know will be a game changer for you. Now you will consciously know your strengths and can work to sharpen them while also being aware of your weaknesses. You can sharpen those skills as well; start by studying and emulating others who are proficient in your weaker areas. Ask questions to find out *why* they operate the way they do, then *how* they do what they do!

When I played football, I knew there were always ten other guys on the field with me. Each of us had strengths and weaknesses, but together as a team, or unit, we were solid. While with the team, I had a chance to develop and grow stronger all the way around. I did this by studying and practicing with the others, as you will, too, as you follow along.

Regardless of the setting you are in, just remember: first things first. Know what you know and know what you don't know.

COURSE WORKSHEET NO. 1

List the top ten principles/philosophies you learned from sports:

1. _____

2. _____

3. _____

4. _____

5. _____

6. _____

7. _____

8. _____

9. _____

10. _____

PLAY ONE: WORKSHEET /TEST

(Write your answer to each question in the space provided.)

1. What did you learn from this "How to Transition Like a Champion" chapter that you can take and apply right now in your sport, your life, and/or your business?

   _____

   _____

   _____

   _____

2. Why is transitioning correctly crucial to success?

   _____

   _____

   _____

3. What is carryover?

   _____

   _____

   _____

4. Where do you find carryover?

   _____

   _____

   _____

5. What else can you control besides your attitude?

   _____

   _____

SLB EXTRA POINT

Always remember: doubt takes you out of action, but action takes you out of doubt.

2
THREE THINGS YOU CAN'T MISS

There are a lot of things you will miss in life, but I want to give you three that you can't miss. If you miss any or all of these three, success will elude you. There is no getting around these if you are serious about your next phase of life. I had to learn these along the way in my own experience, but I'm sharing them to make sure you have access to them. This is so you can't say, "I didn't know" or "No one ever told me that." These are three things that molded you in your sport, and it's possible you weren't aware of them—until now. If you apply these three things with the same tenacity, focus, and energy as you did to your sport, nothing can stop you.

Directions: As you go through each section of this book, make the correlation to how each concept relates to you, then figure out how you can apply each in your sport, your life, and your business.

1. PHILOSOPHIES

The philosophies you now have, as well as the ones you have had and will later have, are crucial to your life and chances for success.

A lot of times you hear that your attitude is everything. This is pretty much true, but it's not the only thing. The prerequisite for having the right attitude is having the right philosophy.

Your philosophy (a basic system, knowledge, or set of principles that guide you) will set the tone for your life. It can make you or break you. Most people don't understand how important having the right philosophy is until later in life. That's after everything that could go wrong has gone wrong, and you resort to blaming others for your lack of success. You feel that everyone is luckier than you and has it easier than you, when really the only thing people might have on you is their philosophy or philosophies.

The first question you should ask yourself: What are my philosophies? When I was growing up, I had my own little sayings that often guided my outlook and attitude on life. My brother and I would just say things like "Hope for the best, expect the worst" or "Expect the unexpected." This way we were never surprised about outcomes.

One I used a lot, and which I once heard in a song was, "If I ever fall, spring back like a rubber band." Another one: "I ain't worried about it, God got it." I didn't just say them, I took them to heart. Notice how simple these are; just a few words, easy to remember. When I say "philosophy," I don't mean something that takes pages to explain: keep it simple. These philosophies empowered me to be relentless, to keep pushing when I was down and not to worry about it; it's in God's hands. I never thought a song and sayings would stick with me for life and help me endure as much as these philosophies have.

You can acquire the right or wrong philosophies from anywhere—from people, from music, from the things you let feed your mind. It's important that you control what goes into your head because it will shape and mold your philosophies, whether you know it or not. That's how you can go through life with disempowering philosophies and end up playing the blame game.

Your philosophies will control your attitude, and in turn your attitude will control your actions. Do yourself a favor, get your mind right.

2. ATTITUDE

You can control your attitude. There are many things in life that you're unable to control, but your personal attitude isn't one of them. Most people aren't taught this lesson; therefore, pay close attention if you want to know the key ingredient that determines your attitude and helps you control it. This ingredient is your philosophy. This alone will determine what you think and how you think. In turn, it will determine what you see, which dictates your feeling or position about a topic, which in turn shapes your attitude toward it.

The word "attitude" already has a negative connotation, and a negative attitude will get you nowhere. Have you ever heard the saying, "A change in attitude is a change in latitude?" Well, it suggests that a good attitude will take you a long way, even to the top. Your attitude can put you in position to win in sports, life, or business; it also can put you in position to lose.

Understanding this is crucial, because your attitude is often what separates the successful from the unsuccessful, regardless how you personally define success. Anything can happen to anybody, but the people with a positive (or right) attitude about what has happened to them tend to respond in an effective manner, which creates a favorable outcome or at least prevents the situation from worsening. People with the wrong or bad attitude tend to react negatively, which creates the opposite effect.

Your attitude will ultimately determine the actions you take.

3. ACTION

Actions are where the rubber meets the road. Your actions are where you make it happen, or where your inaction lets random events, or fate, determine the outcome. You can only do so much in sports, in life, or in business before it comes down to your taking action. Your action(s) will be greatly influenced by your philosophies and your attitude. Those two things will ultimately determine the course of your actions—good, bad, right, wrong, fast, slow, empowering, disempowering, etc.

When you act, don't just take any action, take *massive action*. Massive action is the activity that takes you from where you are in your sport, life, or business to where you want to be. The right attitude and philosophies are what keep you there.

Two things will prevent you from making it to where you want to be in sports, life, or business: (1) not taking enough of the right actions, or (2) not having the right philosophy and attitude to push you along the way.

Once everything is said and done, you want to look back and know that you did whatever it took (ethically) to make it. Don't be the person who says they did what it took while knowing deep down they could have done more, and now they must live with that pain of regret. The pain of disappointment is temporary; the pain of regret lasts forever.

Do not be the person who didn't have the right philosophy and attitude, and that's what made their actions fall short.

COURSE WORKSHEET NO. 2

Think back to and consider the lessons, principles, and philosophies you have found from sports that correlate and list at least TEN that you can APPLY to life and/or business.

1. _____

2. _____

3. _____

4. _____

5. _____

6. _____

7. _____

8. _____

9. _____

10. _____

PLAY TWO: WORKSHEET/TEST

1. What did you learn from the "three things you can't miss" (philosophies, attitude, actions) segments that you can apply right now to your sport, life, or business?

   _____

   _____

   _____

   _____

2. What are the three things you can't miss?

   1. _____

   2. _____

   3. _____

Three Things You Can't Miss

3. From where or who can you acquire philosophies? Circle answer(s).

    A. People

    B. Music

    C. Books

    D. TV

    E. Anywhere

4. Your attitude is not controllable. True or False? Explain why.

    _____

    _____

    _____

5. Nothing influences your actions. True or False? Explain why.

    _____

    _____

SLB EXTRA POINT

Being where you are might not be your fault, but staying there will be.

3
LIFE HAPPENS

GOOD, BAD, OR UGLY—THAT'S HOW LIFE UNFOLDS FOR MOST OF US. The next phase of your life might not come as easy as the first. What will you do to make the most of it? Maybe it will comfort you to know that when things are going bad for you, similar things have gone wrong for others, if not worse.

Instead of feeling down and looking for an excuse to quit when circumstances are beating you up, or maybe you want someone to feel sorry for you, find a reason to keep going, to overcome. Only you can do this for yourself. Life is sometimes going to happen in a manner not to your liking; knowing this in advance will protect you from being caught off guard. This is when you must figure out how to make things work and just move on. In my book *What's Next?*, I go into a lot more detail on this subject, relating it to my own life experiences.

Directions: As you go through each section of this book, make the correlation to how each concept relates to you, then figure out how you can apply each in your sport, your life, and your business.

LBYP (LIVING BELOW YOUR POTENTIAL)

This is an affliction more common than the common cold, and it spreads faster than a cancer. This just might be the most common yet mysterious disease ever discovered in human existence.

Symptoms of LBYP

- Being OK with being OK
- Doing the bare minimum
- Settling for less
- Conforming vs. transforming
- Not having goals
- Making excuses
- Blaming others
- Letting life happen

The way I see it, LBYP is the most common disease on Planet Earth; it has claimed more lives than any other scourge known to man. It's been around since the beginning of humanity. For centuries, it went undiagnosed. Even though it has been identified, LBYP has no cure—it can't be treated with medication, so doctors cannot help you. Your parents can't help because they probably suffered from it as well—without knowing what it was or even being aware that they had it—before passing it on to you at birth. This disease will claim your life as well unless you decide to fight it.

You are probably wondering how to fight this terrible disease. Well, first, you need to perform a self-diagnosis. Ask yourself these two questions. 1. Am I where I want to be in life? 2. Did I do everything in my power daily to get me to where I want to be? If you answered no to the first question, then refer to the symptoms listed above. If you answered no to the second question, you are suffering from full-blown LBYP—Living Below Your Potential. If you answered no to both questions, then your dreams and hopes are dead. You have already given up on life and really have only two options: wake up and get your life back or die from LBYP.

Life Happens

LBYP awareness check: Based on your own sports, life, or business experiences, answer the following questions:

1. Are you suffering from LBYP?

   _____

2. How can you get it?

   _____

   _____

   _____

3. What actions can you take daily to beat LBYP?

   _____

   _____

   _____

4. What are your most common symptoms?

   _____

   _____

PRIDE POLICY

Do you have a pride policy?

Rule of thumb: Make sure you have enough pride to go after any desire you choose to pursue, but you also will need enough humility to know when you need assistance. Never have so much pride that you can't swallow it. A lot of times you can find yourself suffering from LBYP because your pride is in the way and you won't allow yourself to ask for help.

You need to have the pride to start dreaming big, setting goals, and taking action, but at some point, when the challenge becomes more than you can handle, it's time to surrender your pride and seek wisdom or find a mentor.

Most of the time you are fighting battles you can't win alone, but you are caught up in self and your own personal pride. You never take the time to consult with someone who's seasoned, prepared, or been where you are looking to go. You should go to them to get that assistance that you needed a long time ago and which would have saved you time, energy, and money.

Don't let your pride prevent you from using your TEAM that is there to assist you. In sports, in life, and in business, Together Everyone Achieves More (TEAM).

You might think you must do things yourself when you don't. You believe you are in it alone when you are not! What is your pride policy? If you don't have one, let's create one for you!

ACHIEVEMENTS GIVE HOPE

It's incredible when you realize that life isn't really about you.

Nothing you do is really about you, even though you benefit from it or are otherwise affected by it along the way. Achievements giving

Life Happens

hope is obvious, in everything; all you have to do is look around and notice your achievements or achievements of others.

Do your past or current achievements give other people hope? Or have you ever been given hope by seeing someone achieve a goal or accomplish something monumental? If you answered yes to either of these, seeing others achieve their dreams and goals gives you hope that you can achieve your dreams and goals. Achievements are *for* you, but they are not *about* you. I say this because someone is always watching you. If you don't believe me, just think back to when you were always watching someone and most likely still are.

Your purpose is bigger than you, because what you are doing is giving others hope that they can be more. They can see more, they can do more, they can achieve more. At some point, someone gave you that hope, now it's your turn to pass it along.

You have to take a hard look at *why* you do what you do, because when it's all said and done, you want to make sure there has been more done than said.

COURSE WORKSHEET NO. 3

List six personal scenarios in sports that are examples of the principles/philosophies of life happening, pride getting in the way, and achievements giving hope:

1. _____

2. _____

3. _____

4. _____

5. _____

6. _____

PLAY THREE: WORKSHEET/ TEST

1. What did you learn from the discussion about LBYP that you can apply right now to your sport, life, or business?

   _____

   _____

   _____

Life Happens

2. What does LBYP mean?

   _____

3. Having no goals is not a symptom of LBYP. True or False?

   _____

4. You should always let your pride take over. True or False? Explain.

   _____

   _____

   _____

5. Your achievements inspire only you. True or False? Explain why.

   _____

   _____

   _____

SLB EXTRA POINT
It's the philosophies that make the actions work.

4
THE CHOICE IS YOURS

MAKE IT A POINT TO ALWAYS REMEMBER THE LINE "THE CHOICE is yours." In terms of success in your next chapter of sports, life, or business, the choice also is yours. You need to know, "If it is to be, it's up to me, not friends, family, employer, partners, or teammates." Good, bad, ugly, indifferent . . . either you take life as it happens or you make life happen. The choice is yours.

Whether you commit first and figure it out later, or you spend forever trying to figure it out, the choice is yours. To do or to not do in sports, life, and business, the choice is yours. Not only is the choice yours, the outcome is also yours.

The saying "The choice is yours" brings out responsibility for you in your sport, life, and business, However, some people are not ready to accept responsibility for their choices or even the responsibility for having to make a choice. Just remember your sport; it's likely you are highly trained in the area of making choices in a split second, so the same applies.

Regardless if you make a choice or not, you will be responsible for the outcome. So, you might as well operate like the choices are yours when your time comes. You can make those choices that determine the outcome of your life and business while also impacting the people that will follow you based on your choices.

Directions: As you go through each section of this book, make the correlation to how each concept relates to you, then figure out how you can apply each in your sport, your life, and your business.

NO HOPE TO NEW HOPE

Every second of the day, every time you breathe, you get a chance to go from no hope to new hope. This is true as long as you don't quit. I found myself in this position twice in life. The first time was when I tore my ACL my senior year of high school and had no clue how I was going to accomplish my goal of getting a scholarship to a D1 school in the SEC to play football—but it happened. The second was when I started my sales career after college, I started out doing really well for three months and then the slow season came. Not understanding the sales game or being financially literate, I found myself in the worst position I had ever been in as an adult—with an overdrawn bank account. That was a wakeup call. Four months later I was nominated as a top salesperson for my sales team, and I stayed one for the next seven years, until I left the industry.

If things aren't going the way you want them to go, if they aren't looking how you want them to look, ask yourself, "What am I going to do with this moment, with the next opportunity to do something about it?" The next second can change your life for better or for worse. Just like sports, you can go from zero to hero or vice versa in one play, so don't fret, because you have been in this situation before.

What are you going to do, to go from no hope to new hope? Don't expect help until you are willing to help yourself.

Will you maximize that next opportunity to go from no hope to new hope? Every second you are alive should give you that little bit of hope that you can change your life. Make that extra call, do that extra interview, go to that extra networking event, do that extra rep, get that extra practice, invest that extra time, go that extra mile. If you still have life, you can change your life. Remember that.

Life is a series of moments, and any moment could be your defining moment to go from no hope to new hope! I again refer you to my book *What's Next?* to read my story.

OPT OUT

For a while I kept getting this promotional email, and it made me realize something: a lot of the things you are going through (or getting via email) in life, you signed up for. That's on you. Think about your sport and how you went through the ranks; then there was the food you had to opt out of eating; then the friends you had to opt out of being friends with; and then the other things you had to opt out of so you could focus on being the best. This will not change in life or business.

Have you ever gotten emails and over time you realized that the content of the email wasn't beneficial to you anymore—the emails were just taking up space in your in-box? The same thing will happen with people, relationships, habits, hobbies, and other things in life. When you realize this, you need to opt out of that subscription.

When you don't add value to people, places, or situations, or they no longer add value to you, it might be time to consider opting out.

You deal with it, you let it bring you down, you let it hold you back, and all you really needed to do was opt out of it. So next time you think about unnecessary things you're facing, all you must do is opt out. The choice is yours.

WHAT AM I *NOT* DOING

Day by day you speed through life, staying busy. You are doing this, you are doing that. Most of the time you are doing what you believe you need to be doing to get to where you want to go. From my own experience, I came to realize that it's probably not the things you *are* doing, it's the things you *are not* doing that are preventing you from getting to where you want to go. Remember the drill you used to do in practice, and it was your first time doing it, but, for whatever reason, your coach made you do it over and over until you produced the outcome that he wanted. You would begin to get frustrated and then you would ask the magical question, "What am I not doing?" Did that ever happen to you, or was that just me?

Sometimes you must do a self-assessment. You know what you are focused on doing now, and you know what you are doing next—you got that figured out. However, there might be a missing piece and you need to ask yourself what it could be.

What am I not doing that could be holding me back?

What am I not doing that might be preventing me from my desired outcome?

What am I not doing that is important?

Or, maybe you are doing it, but just not enough of it. Whatever it is, it could be the missing ingredient, the missing piece, the x-factor, or whatever you want to call it. It could be what you need for advancement.

If you are running a play but the play is not turning out the way the coach drew it up, it's probably because you're missing an ingredient or at least a certain amount of the ingredient. In turn, adjustments are made to add or take away from the play to get the desired outcome.

So, what it all boils down to is that you might have to reevaluate your recipe if you're not getting the desired outcome. Look at the people who are getting the outcome you want; if you're using the same ingredients, it should be only a matter of time before you get the same outcome. This might help you find what you are missing. The next time you look around, ask yourself, "What am I *not* doing?"

COURSE WORKSHEET NO. 4

List three things that come to your mind for which you need to make better choices, then three things you need to opt out of, and, finally, three things you are not doing that could be hindering your success:

1. _____

2. _____

3. _____

1. _____

2. _____

3. _____

1. _____

2. _____

3. _____

PLAY FOUR: WORKSHEET/TEST

1. What did you learn in this "Life Happens" chapter that you can take and apply right now in your sport, life, or business?

   _____

   _____

   _____

   _____

2. What's happening to you will only happen to you, and everyone else has it better. True or False? Explain why.

   _____

   _____

   _____

3. List the two determining factors that decide if you should opt out?

   1. _____

   2. _____

The Choice Is Yours

4. How many opportunities do you get to go from no hope to new hope?

   _____

5. The problem is always what you are doing. True or False? Explain.

   _____

   _____

   _____

SLB EXTRA POINT

Find an excuse to keep going, not an excuse to give up.

5
KNOW THE GAME

IF YOU DON'T KNOW THE GAME, HOW CAN YOU PLAY IT? MORE IMPORTANTLY, how can you win at it? The game of sports, life, and business is about winning. To win, though, you must know the objective.

In sports, the rules and regulations and objectives are laid out for you. In life and business, they are not; everything depends on the type of life and business in which you are involved. You would not play your sport without knowing the rules of the game, so why would you enter a new game without taking the time to learn the rules of life and business? This section is designed to make sure you keep this in mind—knowing the game—in whatever game you are playing, play to win. Knowing the game puts you ahead of the game, and it allows you to put yourself and others in position to win.

Directions: As you go through each section of this book, make the correlation to how each concept relates to you, then figure out how you can apply each in your sport, your life, and your business.

RULES & REGULATIONS

Know the game and play it well.

How can you play the game if you don't know the rules? Well, it's a fact that you can play the game without knowing the rules, but it's doubtful you will win it. With this game, I'm talking about the rules and regulations of sports, life, and business. When you think about your sport, did knowing the rules help you play with more confidence because you knew exactly what you could and couldn't do to win?

Whatever game you feel applies to you, ask yourself: "Do I know the rules and regulations and how to put myself and my team, or family, or company, in the best position to win and not get penalized for it?" That's half the problem you will face today.

If you are not having the success you want, you could be playing a game for which you do not know the rules. That's playing with an intent to lose and then wondering why you did lose.

The question you must ask yourself: "Do I know the rules and regulations to my game?" If you don't, learn them or play at your own risk. If you don't know them, you will not win, and you will consistently feel like someone has the upper hand and you are being set up to lose. The game will seem difficult, when actually it's simple, but you did not take the time to learn how to play it and, even more importantly, how to win it.

Remember to never get mad at a game you played and lost if you never learned the rules and regulations.

SEEK WISDOM

One time I was reading the Bible, and I came across Scripture about the wise men. As I read the Bible, every few chapters I came across the phrase "seek wisdom." I saw those words so much that they began to stand out to me. So, I broke it down.

Take a look at it yourself; you got the word "wis," which is the root for "wise." The Bible is clearly telling you to seek wise words, thoughts, actions, or people. That's the aim, and if you miss that message on seeking advice from the wise, or the "wis," you are just left with "dom." I'm not calling anyone dumb, but just think about the sport you played and coaches and players who came before you that you had a chance to learn from—ask them for advice, because they have been where you are looking to go. They are like an open book for the test you are bound to take. How wise would it be to consult with people who have experiences in other areas of life and business so you can be prepared for the test ahead as well? Or would you rather go into those tests/situations blindly? That's the price you pay if you don't seek wisdom.

How do you seek wisdom? Get advice, read books, learn from those who have been where you are looking to go and who are living the way you want to live. These are people carrying themselves the way you want to carry yourself. These are people who have the types of relationships you want to have.

BRING IT ALL TOGETHER

One thing we often do not do is retain and utilize what we have learned throughout the course of our lives, from preschool to grade school to college to careers. It is the ability to take those lessons, principles, and philosophies from different experiences in time and bring them all together for the advancement of where we are now. We should also have discernment regarding what lessons, principles, and philosophies to *not* carry over, because they were detrimental in the past.

What you will see here are some principles that are taught but overlooked and others that are taught but are no longer relevant. On the other hand, some principles are *more* relevant than ever in sports, in life, or in business.

A lot of these principles that you have learned or were taught could be ones that can help you get ahead. Or, they also could be outdated ones that are holding you back. Learn with discernment. "How do you do that?" It's simple: First, list the areas of success you have had. Then list the mind-set, principles, or philosophies you applied that gave you the outcome you desired. Next, list the areas of failures you had. Now list the mind-set, principles, or philosophies applied to get that outcome. Somewhere in this equation you will notice that the formula changed. Whether it was confidence, doubt, preparation, knowledge, hunger, or the lack thereof, etc., something changed. Second, you can interview multiple people who have experienced the success you desire and make a list of the common principles or philosophies they embrace and use to create their success.

By the time you complete this program, you will be able to decide which principles you need to bring together and implement in your sport, your life, or in your business.

How do you bring it all together? Take the principles you have learned and see how they can benefit you in another area right now. Also, see if any of the current principles you are applying are holding you back in any area(s) of your sport, life, or business.

SELL OUT

To win in sports, you have to sell yourself out to your craft.

A "sellout" is probably something you've never wanted to be called. Being labeled a sellout usually has negative connotations, something to be frowned upon, something that carries a "loser-ish" label.

Nowadays, when it comes to being successful in sports, life, or business, you're required to "sell out"—that is, to be "all in" on something, to do whatever it takes, to go all in, to burn all bridges, to know there is no turning back.

Those things in sports, life, and business that are worth having and worth achieving at some point will require you to sell out to attain them.

In sports, that's leaving it all on the court, field, track, pool, or wherever your sport is played, knowing you gave everything you had. In

Know the Game

life, that's sacrificing, compromising, improvising to make the marriage work. In business, that's putting it all on the line and saying there is no turning back. You are going all in; this is your Plan A through Plan Z.

When you hear about your products selling out, it's a great thing. It means there is high demand for what you have; everyone wants it. That's what you must mimic—become that high-demand commodity where everyone wants you, your services, or your products.

Before you can sell out your services or products, you must sell out yourself. Be all in with your belief. You are raised and brought up to not be a sellout, but when you look at the clues of the successful, only the sellouts get everything they desire out of life, although I acknowledge we are talking about two different uses of sell out/sellout.

So, will you sell out or not? The choice is yours!

COURSE WORKSHEET NO. 5

1. What is the new "game" you are striving to play? (ex: father, husband, employee, manager, entrepreneur)

   _____

2. List the core rules to that game you need to know to put yourself in position to win at that game.

   _____

   _____

   _____

   _____

3. In which areas of your new game do you need to seek wisdom?

   _____

   _____

   _____

   _____

Know the Game

4. What lessons, principles, or philosophies have you learned from your sport that you can carry over to your new life to help you get ahead?

_____

_____

_____

_____

_____

5. What outdated lessons, principles, or philosophies are you using that are holding you back?

_____

_____

_____

_____

_____

Sports Life Business: The Transition PlayBook

6. List the last three times you sold out in sports, life, or business, and the outcome of each.

   1. _____

      _____

   2. _____

      _____

   3. _____

      _____

PLAY FIVE: WORKSHEET/TEST

1. What did you learn in the "Know the Game" chapter that you can apply right now in your sport, life, or business?

   _____

   _____

   _____

2. You have to know the _____ game to _____ it and _____ it.

3. List a situation that required you to seek wisdom in sports.

   _____

   _____

4. List three lessons, principles, or philosophies that apply to you, and how they correlate in sports, life, and business.

   1. _____

   2. _____

   3. _____

5. What does it mean to sell out?

_____

_____

_____

SLB EXTRA POINT

Don't worry about the odds, because others don't determine success, you do!

6
THE TRANSITION

TRANSITIONING IS SOMETHING YOU DO IN DIFFERENT STAGES OF LIFE even if you never bother to consider the key factors that comprise an efficient and successful transition. Everything we have covered so far in this book will help you transition like a champion, but there are some specific detailed principles that you can apply during your transition. There were a few things while transitioning that allowed me to maximize my transitions, and I'm sure they will work for you as well.

Directions: As you go through each section of this book, make the correlation to how each concept relates to you, then figure out how you can apply each in your sport, your life, and your business.

RUN YOUR VISION

You are on a mission, and what's this mission? To run *your* vision. What do I mean by "run your vision"? I mean doing things and being the person you envision yourself to be.

Strive and work toward the image of what you want to be. Achieve those goals that you believe you were put here to accomplish. This is also known as fulfilling your purpose, completing the job just like you did in sports.

Running your vision is giving yourself permission to create the life you see for yourself. Don't worry about what others think you should do with your life. Do what you believe you were called to do. A lot of times we do things that are socially pleasing just because it is easy, has benefits, pays well, etc. Maybe it was the best option you had at the time, because you were operating out of that fear of not knowing what's next.

Maybe you have spoken with someone close to you about your vision, and they shot yours down because they had no vision and could not see things big enough to see yours. Just know that everyone will not see what you see; that's why it's your vision, not theirs. Don't be dismayed by this. Trust in your vision—no one knows or sees it better than you do.

Wherever this message meets you in your life, just know your time is now. Your opportunity is here. Your best days are ahead if you let go of the past, look forward to the future, and start using the skills, principles, and philosophies that help you become the person you need to be to fulfill the mission for your life and help you run your vision.

How do you run your vision? First, find your vision/purpose. Then study everything (mentors, books, relationships) that can educate you and put you in position to take *massive action* for fulfilling your vision/purpose. Just like it was taught through sports, determine the outcome you want and do everything (practice, film study, train) to get that outcome.

THE FOLLOW-THROUGH

I have to admit; I learned the skill of the follow-through not only from tackling drills but also from chasing girls. I didn't even realize I was learning a skill; I thought I was just having fun. Sure enough, I learned something that I could apply in sports while playing football, in life, and down the road in business.

The Transition

Let me explain what I mean by follow-through and how I learned it in college. I'd be out and about, and whenever I met females and hit it off with them, we would exchange phone numbers. Sure enough, I would call or text them at some point, but sometimes things wouldn't work out. It could be she simply didn't want to respond, or she had a boyfriend, or whatever the case might be.

Instead of losing contact completely, though, I would still periodically reach out just to make contact with her. Over a period of time—it could be days, weeks, months, or even the course of an entire school year—at some point we would finally speak again (in most cases). With that being said, we'd eventually establish a relationship, whether that meant becoming acquaintances or maybe even true friends. My following through and staying consistent allowed this to happen.

Who could imagine doing stuff that you don't expect will affect your life, only for it to become the foundation of a skill set that changes your life? I could apply it to sports, life, and business. That's why I'm a firm believer that there are actions we can take and daily encounters we can engage in to better ourselves. We must be conscious of them because every moment is a learning moment.

The follow-through made me consistent enough to take what my coaches were telling me in the off-season and seeing how I could apply it to week one, then week two, etc. until it was a habit. Following through on those things made me more consistent and shortened my learning curve week in and week out when it came to being prepared for our opponents.

The follow-through also helped me in business; this was the major payoff for the skill set I'd learned. I was always active in the community and would meet people on a regular basis, making great connections. I realized that people were eager to help out and connect me with others in their network. So, after initial meetings, I'd keep in contact every so often to check in on that person. This helped build and strengthen our relationship, even while not knowing if we would ever need each other's assistance. Sure enough, days, weeks, months, or sometimes years later, we would finally have reason to do business or provide a service for one another. The follow-through put me in position to capitalize in college, in the game, and in business.

I learned a valuable lesson just doing what I thought was fun. I challenge you and question you to see what lessons you are learning day-to-day that you could use to change your life in other areas, like the follow-through did for me.

EFFICIENT OPERATION

Do not let your situation determine your operation; we do that most of the time. Have you honestly ever thought about that? Think about your sport: How often has the situation (score) determined your operation (how hard you played)?

What if you approach your daily operations—wherever and whatever they might be—with that same sense of urgency, eagerness, and zeal of "this has to happen or else" desperation mentality day in and day out? What if this was the only operation you worked by? How much more efficient, effective, and successful would you be?

If you operated this way consistently, there is a great chance that you wouldn't ever be in a desperate situation where it was . . . "this has to happen or else."

You can prevent the "I've got to make this happen right now" situation if you approach *every* situation like "I have to make it happen" right now. This keeps you ahead of the curve and keeps you from being painted into a corner timewise. To operate at this level, you need true-to-life urgency in everything you do. This way, you will never have to default into the "just get by" lifestyle in which you find out you weren't doing enough to get by. Now it's a state of desperation,

The Transition

and your back is against the wall, which is not an ideal situation to be in, but is often our most productive time.

Answer me this: does it make sense to do what you've been doing, only to find out down the road it wasn't enough to win the game, and it's too late? Decide to do more right now so that you do not put yourself in position to lose it all. If you are not all in at all times, then your situation is determining your operation. When you are ahead, do you relax? When you are behind, do you push?

Why not operate like you are behind from day one? So now when you are operating at such a high level, you never have to put yourself in that predicament where your level of operation has to change your situation, because your situation is being determined by your level of operation. You are in control of your sport, your life, and your business at this level.

You will have been operating at that game-changer level the whole time, so when it's time to change the game, you never have to change what you are doing. That's because the intensity level people operate at during desperation will be your new normal. You have changed the game from day one by operating at a higher level.

Operate like you are in desperation mode all the time, so if the situation ever gets bad, you are ahead of it. From this day forward, resolve to not let your situation determine your operation; instead, determine your situation by the level of your operation, and this should be your motivation.

COURSE WORKSHEET NO. 6

1. What is it that you believe makes transitioning difficult?

   _____

   _____

   _____

2. What is the biggest challenge you have experienced while transitioning?

   _____

   _____

3. Have you ever compared the challenge you listed above in No. 2 to an identical challenge in your sport? Why or Why not?

   _____

   _____

   _____

   _____

The Transition

4. Correlate your biggest challenge to a challenge in your sport that you experienced. (Think of it this way: This challenge is the same as that challenge, and this is why.)

_____

_____

_____

_____

_____

PLAY SIX: WORKSHEET/TEST

1. What did you learn in this "Transition" chapter that you can apply right now in your sport, life, or business?

   _____

   _____

   _____

2. What goes into having an effective transition?

   _____

   _____

   _____

3. What does it mean to run your vision?

   _____

   _____

   _____

The Transition

4. What determines how most people operate?

   _____

   _____

   _____

5. Your situation should always determine your operation. True or False? Explain why.

   _____

   _____

   _____

SLB EXTRA POINT

Success ingredients: purpose + hope x massive action.

7
MASTER THE MIND-SET

IF YOU DON'T MASTER THE RIGHT MIND-SET, THE WRONG MIND-SET will master you. That's a recipe for disaster, just in case you didn't know. There are a lot of things that you see, you hear, you do, that help mold your mind-set on many different topics. I want to make sure you are equipped with some knowledge that will help you determine what you allow to mold and condition your mind-set. As part of this process, I want you to master *who* you are without the game—as a nonathlete. It's simple; you have mastered the mind-set that made you an athlete—now just do it again, but in a different phase of your life. When it comes to mind-set, remember to take the mind-set that made you thrive in your sport and approach the next phase of life and business with the same mind-set and build it to sharpen it from there.

Directions: As you go through each section of this book, make the correlation to how each concept relates to you, then figure out how you can apply each in your sport, your life, and your business.

PICK YOUR PERSPECTIVE

Your perspective is guaranteed to do one of two things: empower you or imprison you.

Vision will determine what you see; your perspective will determine how you see it.

The interesting thing about perspective is that you can adopt the perspective that makes you feel good about yourself, your situation, your problems, and about whatever you are dealing with. Or you can adopt the perspective that empowers you to change your situation—which is a principle you learned in sports although the concept is a subconscious teaching, so you do not know that it is what you are learning.

You can get further, push longer, and push harder in life and business if you adopt the perspective that empowers you to push for change versus adopting the perspective that makes you feel good and allows you to settle for just being OK—for just getting by, for losing at life or business, for quitting on your dreams, hopes, and family because everyone else seems happy.

Your aim should be to adopt the perspective that's going to make you man up or woman up, be more, do more, push for more, and expect more, and ultimately receive more. It's the same perspective your coaches have regarding you; that's how they got the most out of you as a player in your sport. This is the same perspective you must apply to life and business to get the most out of yourself and to achieve what you can achieve.

At the end of the day, it's all about picking your perspective. I encourage you to pick the one that pays the most! Pick the one that empowers you!

LEGENDARY CONVERSATION

When you are talking with your friends, family, inner circle, mentor . . . whoever it might be, and you share your innermost desires about sports, life, or business—these are what I consider legendary conversations. A legendary conversation is one in which, once you've gone your separate ways, the seeds from that conversation have been planted and rooted and begun to inspire you or the other person to

Master the Mind-set

make the change, set the goal, take the action, or whatever it might be that drives the creation of making that conversation a reality.

Legendary conversations consist of building up, not tearing down; purpose pushing, not purpose bashing; value adding; and character molding. These are the conversations that become empowering and significant in your life and for others. One day you and whoever it might be will look back and say, "Remember when we talked about this and talked about that? Look at us now."

When speaking with your inner circle, you must ask yourself, "What am I giving them? What value am I adding to their lives from this conversation?" You want every conversation to live on with that person or persons after you are gone.

If you're not having legendary conversations, sit back and evaluate your self-talk, evaluate your conversations. What are you talking about? If you are listening, who are you listening to? Are they adding value? You have two ears and one mouth for a reason, because listening is crucial, but know what you are listening for. What can you take from that conversation that will make you better? You listen to learn; you do not just listen to listen. If that is the case, you are wasting their time and yours.

Talk about stuff that's making a difference; that's what a legendary conversation is about. Aim to make every inner-circle conversation legendary.

COLD, HARD FACTS

The cold, hard facts are just the truth; often in sports it's coming from the coach, and we rarely want to hear it even though we need to hear it.

Here is one of the most important things that school and athletics on any level has done for you; some of you might have capitalized on it and some of you might have not realized it yet. It's not all about what you know; a lot of times it's who you know or who knows you. Relationships can often take you further than knowledge can, but you must have the knowledge to realize it.

High school, college, professional organizations, and organized sports all create a natural network for you. They put you around people with whom you can network, so that later on down the road you can have the connections that are going to put you in a position to win because of people you have met. Many athletes don't capitalize on this position because, although the opportunity is readily available, the social interaction is only surface deep. The conversations you have with people other than your peers are usually about your sport or other sports. You, as an athlete, haven't taken the time to become vulnerable and to let people get to know you as person, or vice versa. Or maybe you avoid meeting or hanging around people who aren't athletes at all, which is even worse. You have a stage and an opportunity to meet all kinds of people from different walks of life; take advantage of it. Make sure your friends group doesn't look just like you. A diverse friends group might put you in position to do what you really want to do in life or in business because of who you know or who knows you, regardless of your skills or lack thereof.

This principle doesn't change even in the next phase of your life, after sports. The question you must ask yourself: "With whom have I been connecting?" Have you been more focused on yourself than on meeting others and shaking hands? The cold, hard truth is that you do not need to know all the facts to get where you want to go in life or in business, but you do need to know the right people. That's the moral to this story; it's all about people—*who you know* and *who knows you* can possibly take you further than *what you know*.

COURSE WORKSHEET NO. 7

1. List the activities you did that allowed you to master the mind-set of being a top athlete.

   _____

   _____

   _____

   _____

2. Write down a situation that left you with an empowering perspective.

   _____

   _____

   _____

3. What do you feel controls and molds your mind-set the most? Has that changed throughout the course of your life?

   _____

   _____

4. Are you engaged in legendary conversations? If so, with whom? If not, why not?

   _____

   _____

   _____

5. Vision determines _____. Your perspective determines _____.

PLAY SEVEN: WORKSHEET/TEST

1. What did you learn in this "Master the Mind-set" chapter that you can apply right now in your sport, life, or business?

   _____

   _____

   _____

2. What should a legendary conversation consist of?

   _____

   _____

   _____

3. By default, you will either master the right mind-set or the wrong mind-set. True or False?

   _____

4. It's not who you know, it's what you know that will help you. True or False? Explain why.

   _____

   _____

SPORTS LIFE BUSINESS: THE TRANSITION PLAYBOOK

_____

_____

5. What are two things your perspective will do to you?

   1. _____

   2. _____

SLB EXTRA POINT

All roads lead to a destination. Are you on the right road?

8
THE BASICS: READING, WRITING & ARITHMETIC

THESE THREE SUBJECTS WERE ESSENTIAL WHEN IT CAME TO HAVING success in school, and I believe they are essential when it comes to success in sports, life, and business. Let me explain why. They are the basics; without the basics, it is difficult to have success in anything. Here you will get to look at how understanding a few basic principles can put you in position to thrive. These basics are some fundamentals you indirectly learned during sports, but now they will be brought to the light, making you more conscious of them and also showing you the value you possess that you probably were unaware of. Although the titles of the skills are basic, the concepts in which they are taught aren't.

Directions: As you go through each section of this book, make the correlation to how each concept relates to you, then figure out how you can apply each in your sport, your life, and your business.

KNOWLEDGE DOES NOT EQUAL POWER

You've heard the expression that "knowledge equals power," something I believed early in my entrepreneurial career. I quickly decided to learn all that I could about people skills and sales as part of my personal development. I put all my extra time into reading and studying my new learned skills with my peers and business partners. There was one little problem, though.

I had been doing everything in my power to add knowledge so I could grow my business, since knowledge equals power—but nothing had changed. I was learning a lot, but my business looked the same. Then one day, listening to an audio book, I heard the answer to my problem.

Knowledge itself does not equal power; the *use of knowledge* equals power! Wow, no one told me that. During all this time that I was acquiring knowledge, I wasn't applying it to my life and business to produce the results I wanted. That's when I thought about football, but it applies to any sport. You can know the play, but if you don't apply what you know to execute the play, then it's just like you do not know the play. You did not become great at your sport because of your knowledge of the game alone; you became great because you were able to use knowledge to help you execute in practice, the game, etc. This is a basic fundamental that the game of sports teaches us, but some of us miss the lesson because we fail to make the correlation.

So now that you know knowledge doesn't equal power, make sure you're getting the proper knowledge on the front end, so you can then take the proper actions throughout your journey. Do not do what I did; work, work, and work until I realized it wasn't working. Instead, take the knowledge you have learned and apply it.

I spent time learning just to learn; nowadays I learn just to apply. I want you to do the same. I'll say it again: knowledge doesn't equal power; the use of knowledge equals power.

ABC'S OR DEF'S

One time while I was looking at the alphabet, I happened to notice some interesting letter combinations that could be applied in sports, life, or business. They were as clear as day: ABC DEF — the first six letters of the alphabet. I suddenly realized something the alphabet had been telling me for years! The interesting thing was that the hint

The Basics: Reading, Writing & Arithmetic

the alphabet is giving us was already being applied daily in my sport and the same is happening in yours. Without these basic lessons, sports wouldn't exist. There would not be "elite athletes" without these elements.

Although they're basic, it's important to know your ABCs—they represent your Actions, your Beliefs, and your Confidence. Without knowing what Actions to take in whatever you are doing, you will not advance.

If you are taking action, the next thing you must do is make sure you are taking the *right* action. This gets you to the letter B, for Belief. Having belief in yourself and in the actions you take will help get you your desired outcome. These actions and beliefs are what will produce your Confidence—Confidence in yourself, your beliefs, your abilities, and in everything you did in sports that got you to your highest level. This has been the basic formula all along, although up until now we had only applied it to our sport. These are basics for success in life and business as well. The absence of action, belief, and confidence in life or business will result in your being stuck with the DEFs of life and business.

The DEFs represent Doubts, Excuses, and Frustration. Without the right ABCs, you will default to the DEFs. First is Doubt; you doubt yourself, your abilities, and what is possible. Once this happens, it will cause you to make Excuses for what you are not doing, why you are not doing it, and why you are not getting anything accomplished. In turn, this will cause you to get Frustrated to the point where you want to quit on yourself, your family, your future, and give up on your hopes, dreams, and aspirations.

Know your ABCs or get stuck with DEFs.

MATH CLASS

As you are going through school, you find that you either love math class or hate it, because math class is all about solving equations that you might or might not ever use again. Most people don't *like* solving math problems in school; well, at least I didn't. I just did it because I had to.

The root of creation/invention is finding a way to solve a problem. Once we get into the real world, we face problem after problem, but often feel like we aren't prepared to handle these problems. We are, but maybe we don't realize it; maybe that is what math class was preparing us for!

If I were told that life is all about being great at problem solving, I would have applied myself more in math class. This way I could have felt more prepared to handle the problems of life. One thing they don't teach you in math class is that the lesson you really need to learn isn't getting the numbers to equal a certain outcome—it's that the act of solving the problem is in itself something you need to be able to do on your own as a life skill.

This made me think about football and sports as whole. This is pretty much what we do—we solve the problem that our opponent is looking to create so that they can score. Or, the other way around, solve the problem the opponent has created that is preventing us from scoring.

What you really need to grasp is that success comes with the ability to be a problem solver. It's not 1+1 equals 2; it's "Do you have the ability to see a problem and offer a solution for that problem in sports, in life, or in business?"

This is the secret to advancement—to become an incredible problem solver in your field just like you were in your sport. There will always be something that has a problem to go with it, but those who master

The Basics: Reading, Writing & Arithmetic

the art of solving problems will be the ones who win in sports, in life, and in business.

You indirectly learn this problem-solving lesson as you go through school because it is a basic success principle, but during math we are never taught to take hold of the reasoning behind the math—and that reasoning involves creating the ability to solve the problems.

COURSE WORKSHEET NO. 8

1. In two to three sentences, explain what "Knowledge is not power" means to you.

   _____

   _____

   _____

   _____

2. In two to three sentences, explain how the ABCs benefit you in sports, life, or business.

   _____

   _____

   _____

   _____

The Basics: Reading, Writing & Arithmetic

3. Describe a time when you suffered from the DEFs in sports, life, or business.

   _____

   _____

   _____

4. How do you feel you were able to apply your problem-solving skills to your sport?

   _____

   _____

   _____

PLAY EIGHT: WORKSHEET/TEST

1. What did you learn in this "Reading, Writing & Arithmetic" chapter that you can apply right now in your sport, life, or business?

   _____

   _____

   _____

   _____

2. What do math class and life have in common?

   _____

   _____

   _____

3. What do the ABCs represent?

   _____

   _____

   _____

The Basics: Reading, Writing & Arithmetic

4. What do the DEFs represent?

   _____

   _____

   _____

5. Knowledge does not equal power. True or False? Explain why.

   _____

   _____

   _____

SLB EXTRA POINT

**You will never be what you want to be,
but you will always be what you work to be.**

9
GO PRO AT LIFE

Y OU PUT ALL YOUR ENERGY, ALL YOUR EFFORTS, ALL YOUR FOCUS, and all your pain and sacrifice into going pro at this game that you love.

This game is the one in which you see guys and gals get crowned as greats for what they did in the game. You put everything into going pro or playing this one game on the highest level and if that one thing doesn't work out, or when your time comes to an end, you feel worthless. Maybe you even feel like a failure, maybe even lost, because this is all you knew, or at least this is what you thought was all you knew.

Or do you feel this way because that is where your identify lies? Have you ever considered all the things you acquired from your sport? Have you ever considered taking these lessons, skills, principles, and philosophies, and then working to be crowned a success from what the game has done for you versus what you did for the game?

Once you are facing life after sports, do not become *hopeless*, become *hopeful*. Do not feel like you failed; feel like you have built your foundation. Do not let up; put on more steam. Push forward to the next phase will allow you to disrupt any opposition . . . just like you did in sports.

All that work you've put into the game has taught you some intangible lessons, skills, principles, and philosophies that will allow you to excel outside of your sport. So, all that work you've been putting in for that fame, and all that work you have been putting in for that name, it will not go in vain unless you let it.

You can still use all that work to go pro at life or go pro in business; you are not limited to sports. The skills you have acquired from sports are just as valuable if not more in the marketplace than in your sports area.

Here is the secret: you have the platform, the philosophies, the strategies, the ideologies, the skill sets, the mind-set you need. The foundation of sports has created all these to help you create what you desire. You just have to decide to put it all together so you can go pro at life and in business. There's more than one way to be a pro.

Directions: As you go through each section of this book, make the correlation to how each concept relates to you, then figure out how you can apply each in your sport, your life, and your business.

I PUT MY LIFE INTO IT

It might feel like your world is over because the game *was* your world, but you will soon see that the game was only a small piece of the world. It looked big only because it consumed you. This type of consumption is what it will take to have success in your next chapter of life or business. This is something I didn't know when I transitioned.

I remember telling myself that there has to be something that covers how to transition from one phase to the next, from high school to college, from college to the real world, or from a pro to an average Joe. I remember the grind I had for the dream of being in that select few that are chosen to go on to the next level. I knew it would take everything I had to make it happen, and at the time I felt like I had put my whole life into manifesting that dream.

I later realized that while I did put my life into it, it was the chase for the dream that put life into me. It gave me the blueprint, the mold, the mental makeup I needed to go and get anything my heart desired. That process was molding me into having a relentless mind-set for achievement and giving me that "You only get one shot" demeanor, to attack life and other endeavors.

Investing your life into something—anything—can cause an identity struggle. I know it did for me, former teammates, and other athletes around the world.

The reason my identity struggle wasn't major and didn't really cause problems for me is because my identity wasn't rooted in the outcome of going pro or being an athlete. My identity was in the creation of who I was becoming as a person and what I could achieve because of the process I had endured as an athlete.

Reread the sentence above! This is the missing link for athletes/people today in sports, in life, or in business who are putting their life into their craft.

So, the question I must ask you is, where is your identity rooted?

SACRIFICE SOMETHING

You've got to be willing to sacrifice the good things for the great things.

This is one thing I realized while at the University of Tennessee. There were a lot of times that my teammates and I sacrificed those good things we all wanted to do as young men in college for the great feeling that came from playing football on Saturday in front of 107,000 fans. We made some of those sacrifices daily and others on a weekly, monthly, or yearly basis.

This doesn't mean we didn't have fun, but there were a lot of good moments we missed out on so that we could experience a few great moments.

These were moments that will be remembered by millions of Tennessee fans and will go down in history. These sacrifices might have stung at the time, and we might have missed some really good college experiences off the field, but they were worth every moment. These are the same types of sacrifices that life requires of us, from starting a family or a new business to beginning a new career and having to sacrifice doing things you want to do, like hanging out with friends. The game has already given you the blueprint for success through the sacrifices you made in your sport, so you know what is required. Now go apply it in the next chapter of your life.

Just know that you must sacrifice what's good to get to great!

ALTER EGO

Growing up, I was told I looked like a thug. As I got older, they said I looked like an athlete. I found it interesting my appearance changed to those around me but the whole time, I saw myself as a king, a leader, a great connector, an entrepreneur, a difference maker.

As time passed, I realized that either you grow to meet people's expectations of you, or you grow until you reach your expectations of yourself.

People will accept or believe either, based on how you act.

This part about expectations is true as you journey through your sport, whether you are playing one sport or multiple sports. This is true as you travel through life, either by yourself or with your family. And it's true as you travel through the workforce as an employee or a business owner. You must realize that it might take your alter ego to help you to become the person you see yourself as. By alter ego, I mean that person inside of you that you truly see yourself as. That person you are meant to become, that person you become when it's crunch time, the game is in your hands, and you must make the play—that is your alter ego.

Go Pro at Life

People will look at you and form an impression of you, and unless you have an alter ego or a strong self-perception of who you are, you will just accept who they say you are and how they treat you. Then you will eventually become what they say you are and conform to their expectations of you, rather than transform to the expectations you have for yourself.

That's where your alter ego kicks in and you show them a person they never saw in you. The question you must ask yourself: "Who is my alter ego?"

SPORTS LIFE BUSINESS: THE TRANSITION PLAYBOOK

COURSE WORKSHEET NO. 9

1. List at least five attributes, skills, lessons, principles, or philosophies you have learned in sports that you feel you can use in life or business.

   1. _____

   2. _____

   3. _____

   4. _____

   5. _____

   6. _____

   7. _____

2. What was the secret I shared with you in this chapter?

   _____

   _____

   _____

3. Why do athletes have identity struggles? Explain.

   _____

   _____

   _____

   _____

PLAY NINE: WORKSHEET/TEST

1. What did you learn from this "Go Pro at Life" chapter that you can apply right now in sports, life, or business?

   _____

   _____

   _____

   _____

2. What three areas can you go pro in?

   _____, _____, and _____.

3. What is an alter ego?

   _____

   _____

4. Either you _____ to meet people's expectations of you or you _____ to reach your own expectations of yourself.

Go Pro at Life

5. What was the key to your not having major identity struggles? Explain.

_____

_____

_____

_____

SLB EXTRA POINT

You can't go uphill with downhill habits.

10
RAISE THE BAR

YOU CAN'T EXPECT TO REACH NEW HEIGHTS IF YOU SET YOUR BAR on the same measurements all your life. There will come a point where you must push yourself, expect more, raise your bar for what you want out of your sport, your life, and/or your business. If you don't raise your own bar, why would you expect someone else to? It's time to think thoughts you've never thought; dream dreams you've never dreamed; read books you've never read; expect things you've never expected. You will never get to that new level until you raise your bar to that level.

Every year in your sport, you strived to get better, but to get better meant you had to win more. And to win more than you did the previous year meant you had to train more and whatever else it took to raise the bar. So, it is the exact same principles, just a different game for you.

Directions: As you go through each section of this book, make the correlation to how each concept relates to you, then figure out how you can apply each in your sport, your life, and your business.

STOP TRYING

Stop trying and start doing.

Consider the statement "Try to read this." Either you read it or you don't. Pretty simple, right? No such thing as try.

Well, if it's that simple, why do you use the word "try" at all? In sports, you either make the play or you don't. You win the game or you lose it. There is no try, just an outcome of defiance. Take it one step further: why is there even such a weak word in your vocabulary?

Strong people do not use weak words, and you are strong because you would not be taking this course if you weren't. You would have already quit on life. It will take that kind of strength to develop a mind-set that does not include such weak words as "try" and "can't" but does include defiant thinking terms such as "I can" and "I will."

This is how it worked for me. Every time I began to say, "I'll try," I thought back to the example I shared with you earlier. What comes to mind for you? It should be either "I'll do it" or "I won't do it." No more *trying* to make it work; either you will or you won't.

Becoming a weak word detective was one of the best things to happen to me. Here is what happened: once I stopped "trying," I started "doing" more. I became more of a producer and less of a procrastinator.

Delete the word "try" from your vocabulary along with any other weak words so that you can stop trying and start doing.

DREAM WITH INTENT TO PURSUE

It's critical that you understand this lesson; a lot of people miss this one. I missed it for years, but when I finally got it, life became so much more focused and intentional.

Do not dream just to dream. Dream with intent to pursue meaning. Dream with the intent of discovering what it will take to make that dream your reality. In your sport, you did not just dream about making it to the highest level you could without putting in any work at the gym. You didn't just dream about winning the championship without taking the actions to produce a championship, did you? Or did you actually follow that dream up with an action plan for attainment? Well, the same rules apply to life and business dreams as well.

No more "I like this," "I like that," or "Well, that would be nice." No more getting stuck in nightmares. How do I define *nightmare*? It's every dream you have that lacks intent or a plan to manifest it.

You would not have that dream if you weren't capable of manifesting it. Stop teasing yourself with these dreams if you do not have an intent to pursue them. Quit wasting time.

This will carry over to everything else you do, which will enable you to operate on higher levels. When you really have intent to pursue something, you won't waste your time doing meaningless things in life or business. You will start to focus on what's worthwhile for attainment of your desire. This will also help you set priorities for the things you are required to handle on a daily basis.

Everything you dream, dream it with the intent to pursue.

3D
DISCIPLINE DISCERNMENT DEDUCTION

I learned a lot of lessons on the football field, but I want to share with you the one that put my life in 3D!

The first lesson was Discipline, which is the most consistent test we face daily. You will succeed or fail on discipline or the lack of it. I learned the art of doing what you are supposed to do versus what you want to do. That's how life will become easier in the long run, yet more tempting in the moment. The art of exercising simple discipline can make your life or break your life. If you don't believe me, just think about the role that discipline played in your sport.

The more discipline you exercise, the more you believe you can put yourself in adverse situations and still make great choices.

This becomes possible once you develop Discernment. This is the second D. It involves using good judgment based on the task at hand. Discernment will spare you from any regrets you might have from making decisions that ignored your discipline boundaries (or good sense). For example, discernment is when you are out with friends having a good time, but the later it gets, the wilder it gets, and you have the presence of mind (discernment) to call it a night and go home before things really get out of hand.

That's what brings out the last and final D—Dedication. This is important because you must be dedicated to the process regardless of the outcome. When you are committed to being the best YOU that you can be, that dedication is what makes you live life in 3D! This is what will keep you from bending, breaking, buckling, or bolting when you face opposition such as people attempting to derail you. Once you dedicate yourself to your course, living life in 3D is what it will take to keep life in 3D and keep you on track, so you can lead by example, and give people someone they can follow.

Raise the Bar

COURSE WORKSHEET NO. 10

1. When was the last time you exercised Discipline, Discernment, and Dedication? Explain.

   _____

   _____

   _____

2. What weak words will you remove from your vocabulary?

   _____   _____

   _____   _____

   _____   _____

3. Name three things you have done in sports to raise the bar and that you can correlate to raising the bar for your life or business.

   1. _____

   2. _____

   3. _____

4. List the dreams you have for yourself that you intend to pursue.

_____

_____

_____

_____

_____

_____

_____

_____

_____

_____

PLAY TEN: WORKSHEET/TEST

1. What did you learn in this "Raise the Bar" chapter that you can apply right now to your sport, life, or business?

   _____

   _____

   _____

2. What should you do to reach new heights?

   _____

   _____

   _____

3. What is defined as a nightmare in this chapter?

   _____

   _____

   _____

4. List the 3Ds.

    1. _____

    2. _____

    3. _____

5. "Stop trying" means to quit. True or False? Explain why.

    _____

    _____

    _____

SLB EXTRA POINT

Be responsible for your happiness.

11
AUDIBLE:
CHECK OMAHA, RIVERSIDE

T HERE ARE TIMES THAT A CHANGE OF PLANS OR DIRECTION IS needed in sports, life, or business. Sometimes you must call an audible, which is a football term for "change the plan" or go in the opposite direction. A lot of times it will just depend on where you are and what's going on, but changes are only an audible away, and you can make the call. Here I will give you some things that might need to happen when you call out "Omaha" or "Riverside"—a couple of well-known (football) audibles—in sports, life, or business.

Directions: As you go through each section of this book, make the correlation to how each concept relates to you, then figure out how you can apply each in your sport, your life, and your business.

REINVENTION

I'll call it reinvention; the art of maximizing change.

I can remember when I started to reinvent myself as a young boy. The reinvention wasn't a planned process; it was a make-the-most-of-it concept that was dropped in my ear by my stepmom.

I didn't quite grasp it at first, but over the course of my first major move at that time, as I got to high school, it registered. I was suddenly part of an unfamiliar environment—its occupants didn't know anything about me, only what they perceived. So, I became what I wanted to be and what I wanted them to see: a star on the football field and in the classroom (this was in high school). It has worked ever since.

In my head, I knew I was born to be great. Teachers and other students didn't know this about me, so it was my job to show them in every aspect possible.

Every time change came, I saw it as an opportunity to increase my greatness and display it at another level. People around me embraced it and perceived it exactly as I displayed it, as I intended it. This reinvention process—change—is the process most people do not know how to take advantage of or to maximize.

Those who do not recognize the moment of opportunity will never maximize the moment and therefore master the art of reinvention.

ENLARGED TERRITORY

At some point, you get to that place where you want more—more out of your sport, more out of your life, more out of your business.

You feel like you are working hard and you are ready to handle more or go on to bigger and better things. It feels like it's taking forever for you to reach that next level. What you must do is ask yourself, "Have I maxed out where I am? Is there still room to grow?"

How can you ask for more when you haven't even maxed out the territory you have? You haven't fulfilled your potential in the here and now, so why are you expecting advancement when you haven't proven yourself?

Oftentimes we ask for something bigger, better, greater when we haven't maxed out what we have. What sense does that make? It's just like sports, when players want more playing time but haven't proved they are reliable or consistent with the time they do get to play.

How can you expect to be giving more, which will require more, when you are not doing everything with what you already have? If you do get more of anything, when you are not ready for it, you definitely won't keep it long. That's true in sports, in life, or in business. A good example is finances. The moment your income exceeds your financial literacy, you had better increase your financial literacy or your income will soon return to the level you are financially prepared to handle.

The size of your territory will never exceed your potential. The only way you can get that enlarged territory is by going all in where you are, with whatever you have available at the time.

The moment you decide to max out your territory where you are with what you've got—to get to where you want to go—is when your territory will be enlarged.

HEAD COACH, OC & DC

At one point while at the University of Tennessee, I wanted to transfer, leave, and put myself in a better situation to play. At least that's what I thought. Come to find out, I was exactly where I was supposed to be. I just hadn't done the work I needed to do to receive the award I was looking for, which is what my coaches told me. So what I found was just like in sports, I believe it's crucial we have a coach in life—someone who can see what we don't see, and someone who can call the plays that put us in position to win.

It's the same thing you will find in life and in business. When things are looking tough, you are right where you're supposed to be, growing through what you're supposed to grow through. That's going to prepare you for where you are heading next although you might not like where you are at that moment.

Even if you don't realize it at the time, or it just seems too tough to bear, you must endure. It's like weight training; the struggle is what builds strength.

Sports Life Business: The Transition PlayBook

Whether it's in sports, life, or business, you might have started off the game falling behind early, but the best thing about the game is you have four quarters, or two halves, or sixty minutes—or whatever the equivalent is in your life or business—to get it right. You can't start over, but you can finish strong. If you make a hard-enough run in the second half, you can still make a comeback and attain whatever it is you are looking to achieve.

You might have started out with some fumbles, missed tackles, picks, and personal fouls, jumped offsides, or missed free throws, or struck out once or twice. But all you need to do is make some adjustments and listen to what your coach in life and business is telling you to do. He or she is putting you in position for your comeback—to make the plays you need to make. That's what great coaches do, but the difference is that great players listen.

COURSE WORKSHEET NO. 11

1. What is the biggest audible you have made at any point in your life?

   _____

   _____

   _____

2. Have you ever exercised the art of reinvention? If yes, how? If no, why not?

   _____

   _____

Audible: Check Omaha, Riverside

3. In two to three sentences, write your understanding of the section "Enlarged Territory."

_____

_____

_____

_____

4. What are your thoughts on having a coach in life and in business?

_____

_____

_____

_____

PLAY ELEVEN: WORKSHEET/TEST

1. What did you learn from "Omaha, Riverside" that you can apply right now to your sport, life, or business?

   _____

   _____

   _____

   _____

2. What is an audible?

   _____

   _____

3. To maximize opportunity, you must what?

   _____

   _____

   _____

4. The size of the territory will _____.

Audible: Check Omaha, Riverside

5. You will always get more to handle before you prove you can handle what you currently have. True or False? Explain why.

_____

_____

_____

_____

SLB EXTRA POINT

You must change your inside before you change your outside.

ABOUT THE AUTHOR

D*ERRICK FURLOW, JR. PLAYED FOOTBALL AT THE UNIVERSITY OF TENNESSEE* and in the Professional Indoor Football League. While at Tennessee, he completed his bachelor's and master's degrees. He is an entrepreneur at heart, speaker, author, and servant to his community. He believes sports are a direct correlation to life and teaches clients everything they need to know to be successful in life and business. Furlow created a place where they all come together in the form of his "Sports Life Business" program for the sole purpose of setting a new standard for how athletes and people transition from one phase of their life to the next! He is living out his purpose here on earth to Impact Inspire & Empower people while setting the new standard for transitioning.

www.ingramcontent.com/pod-product-compliance
Lightning Source LLC
Chambersburg PA
CBHW082127230426
43671CB00015B/2832